Carole Gerber

Spring Blossoms

Illustrated by Leslie Evans

ini Charlesbridge

To Bette Gerber, as she celebrates her
   89th spring—C. G.

To Maeve and Isabella, blossom buddies—L. E.

Published by Charlesbridge
85 Main Street
Watertown, MA 02472
(617) 926-0329
www.charlesbridge.com

Library of Congress Cataloging-in-Publication Data
Gerber, Carole.
   Spring blossoms / Carole Gerber ; illustrated by Leslie Evans.
      p. cm.
   ISBN 978-1-58089-412-8 (reinforced for library use)
1. Flowers—Juvenile literature. I. Evans, Leslie, 1953– II. Title.
QK653.G47 2013
582.13—dc23   2012000791

Printed in China
(hc) 10 9 8 7 6 5 4 3 2 1

Illustrations done in linoleum block print, watercolor, collage, and digital
Display type and text type set in Clearface by International Typeface Corporation
Color separations by KHL Chroma Graphics, Singapore
Printed and bound September 2012 by Jade Productions in Heyuan, Guangdong, China
Production supervision by Brian G. Walker
Designed by Martha MacLeod Sikkema

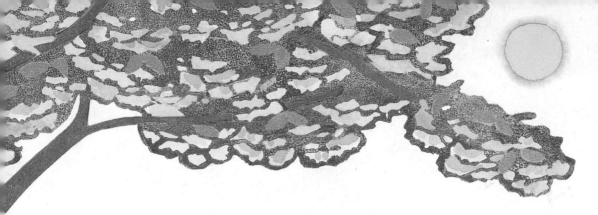

Spring is bursting out all over.
The sun is up. It's warm. Let's go!

Trees, so bare and plain in winter,
are dressed up for their yearly show.

Look at all their buds and blossoms!
Some are pale; some, really bright.

Proudly wearing nature's colors,
spring blossoms sparkle in the light.

White dogwood wears a frosty crown.
Its limbs spread wider than its height.

Crab apple, too, is short and wide,
its fragrant flowers small and white.

Magnolia buds are opening,
revealing blooms that glow like gems.

Cherry flowers grow in bundles,
like small bouquets on long, stout stems.

The white oak bears two kinds of blooms.
Male flowers droop. They're greenish gold.

The female blooms are small and red.
Both open as new leaves unfold.

On the beech, male flowers cluster.
They're round and wear green fuzzy suits.

Female flowers, small and spiky,
grow near the leaves along new shoots.

Red maple tree reflects its name:
both buds and flowers wear red clothes.

The redbud tree does not look red!
Its flowers are a pinkish rose.

White pine's male flowers, small and yellow, grow in clusters near branch tips.

Female flowers bloom weeks later.
They're tinged with red, like slender lips.

Male blossoms grow on balsam fir
beneath its twigs, as we can see.

Their pollen blows to female buds
that grow new cones high on the tree.

Suddenly the trees bend toward us.
A warm spring rain begins to fall.

Wind sets loose a storm of blossoms—
we race around to catch them all!

White dogwood

Crab apple

Magnolia

Cherry

White oak

American beech

Red maple

Redbud

White pine

Balsam fir

In spring the days grow longer. The sun rises higher in the sky, warming the air and ground. This change in temperature signals trees and other plants (as well as many mammals and insects) to awaken from their winter inactivity.

Spring rains soak the soil, releasing minerals and nutrients. Tree roots absorb this liquid and move it up into the tree. There it mixes with a simple sugar the leaves made and stored in the tree during summer and fall. This mixture of water, minerals, and sugar is called sap. Sap moves through the tree, delivering nutrients to its trunk, branches, and buds. The tree grows taller and wider.

Buds, which develop in summer and fall, are dormant in winter. In spring they open into flowers. Many types of trees bear flowers that contain both male parts and female parts. Some have separate male flowers and female flowers on the same tree. Others bear male flowers and female flowers on separate trees.

When pollen produced by the male part falls onto the female part, the flower produces a seed. From these seeds, new trees can grow. Afterward—their purpose complete—the flowers dry up and die. Every spring, this cycle of bud, blossom, seed, and tree repeats itself.